CW00732678

Explaining Deception

Colin Urquhart

Sovereign World

Sovereign World Ltd
PO Box 777
Tonbridge
Kent, TN11 0ZS
United Kingdom

Series editor: Susan Cuthbert

Unless otherwise indicated, all scripture quotations are from the New
International Version, inclusive language version, copyright the
International Bible Society 1999; published by Hodder and Stoughton.

ISBN: 1 85240 344 6

Cover design by CCD, www.ccdgroup.co.uk
Typeset by CRB Associates, Reepham, Norfolk
Printed in the United States of America

Contents

1

The truth

Truth is a person: Jesus Christ. This is a fundamental belief for every true Christian. He is the Word through whom God spoke creation into being. That Word *"became flesh and made his dwelling among us"* (John 1:14).

Jesus came as the light into the spiritual darkness of the world. He came from God the Father *"full of grace and truth"* (John 1:14).

During his earthly ministry, Jesus not only taught about the nature of the kingdom of God, but he made it possible for those who believed to become part of that kingdom, and to receive it as a gift. He gave his life on the cross to enable sinful people to be forgiven and made righteous or acceptable to God.

In our natural state, we are unacceptable to God, for sinners cannot be at one with the holy, righteous God. And *"all have sinned and fall short of the glory of God"* (Romans 3:23). Our sinful condition means that we are condemned to die, to be eternally separated from God.

However, in his love, God has provided a way of escape from the judgment we justly deserve. That way is Jesus. He said:

> *"I am the way and the truth and the life. No one comes to the Father except through me."*   (John 14:6)

Jesus is the *only* way of salvation, the *only* way that we can be saved from the consequences of our sins. Through his death on the cross, he has borne the punishment we deserve, the death penalty. He has offered to his Father the sinless sacrifice of his own life on behalf of sinners – the righteous for the unrighteous, the perfect for the imperfect, the holy for the unholy.

Jesus is the only person ever to be born into the world who has lived a life totally pleasing to God. For ordinary human beings, such a thing is impossible. But Jesus was no ordinary man, for although he was human in every respect he also had a divine nature. He was conceived by God the Holy Spirit within the womb of the virgin Mary. So in his incarnation he was fully God and fully man.

Jesus had a will like any human being, but lived in total submission and obedience to his Father. He lived the perfect life in the power of his divine nature, and offered that perfect life in sacrificial love for us on the cross. We therefore have access to God. Those who believe in Jesus can rightly call God "Father," for they have become his children.

> *Yet to all who received him to those who believed in his name, he gave the right to become children of God – children born not of natural descent, nor of human decision or a husband's will, but born of God.*   (John 1:12–13)

In other words, those who receive Jesus because they believe in him as their Lord and Savior are born again. Jesus made clear that this new birth qualifies a person to receive God's kingdom. Without that new birth, a person remains under condemnation.

Jesus Christ is the only one who has come from heaven, lived on earth and returned to heaven. Every other person begins his or her existence in the mother's womb. But Jesus existed as the Word of God before creation began.

Salvation, total and eternal acceptance in God's sight, is only to be found in Jesus. He alone is the truth; he alone speaks the truth that sets people free from guilt, fears, failure, condemnation, sickness and death. He said:

"If you hold to my teaching, you are really my disciples. Then you will know the truth, and the truth will set you free."

(John 8:31–32)

Jesus made it clear that for our part, only two things are necessary in order to receive the salvation we need and the gift of God's kingdom that he wants to give us. We are to repent and believe.

To repent is more than being sorry for our sins. Many people are sorry about their sins and wished they had not committed them. But they have not necessarily repented.

Repentance involves two things:

1. Not only recognition of sins, but a turning to Jesus who is able to forgive those sins.

2. A complete re-orientation of one's life, a turning away from the old life to embrace a new life. A change of heart and mind, so that now our focus and goals are those the Lord intends for us.

To believe is to put our trust in what Jesus has done for us. This involves a recognition that we could never make ourselves acceptable to God; that we have no way of earning our salvation; that we could never deserve to go to heaven or receive the gift of God's kingdom on our own merit.

To believe is to recognize that Jesus is the sacrifice offered to God on our behalf. We are children of God because of his grace and mercy alone. He identified with our condition by becoming a human being among us; as we trust in him, we are identified with him:

▶ **His righteousness becomes our righteousness.**
▶ **His acceptance becomes our acceptance.**
▶ **His life is the new life we have in him.**

God takes hold of all of those who believe in Jesus, and places them "in Christ Jesus." They now live their lives in him, with his life, power and heavenly resources available to them. As they live under his lordship, so they are able to enjoy all the benefits of his kingdom here on earth, and bear fruit in their lives that will give glory to the Father. They no longer want their own purposes for their lives: their prayer is: "May your kingdom come and your will be done in my life."

The nature of deception

Deception is anything and everything that does not agree with the truth. Jesus is that truth: he is the absolute standard of truth. Deception does not recognize Jesus to be who he is, neither does it accept the total victory he accomplished on the cross. Deception comes from believing anything contrary to what he has said and done.

The Bible is the revelation of that truth. The scriptures record what Jesus has said, what he has done for us, and the inheritance he gives to those who believe in him. Everything thought or said about Jesus or the truth has to be tested against these divinely inspired books.

Anything that does not agree with this revelation of the truth is false; it is error, heresy, deception. God cannot be known by religious speculation, but only through the revelation of the truth.

The Holy Spirit of God gives this revelation to individual people as they seek him. He is the Spirit of truth who guides us into all the truth. Whatever the Holy Spirit reveals will agree with the written revelation of God in the Bible.

God is one, yet reveals himself in three persons: Father, Son and Holy Spirit. This is the mystery of the Trinity. These three persons always agree and they are all equally God. The Son is not less than the Father, neither is the Holy Spirit less than the Father and the Son.

Revelation cannot always be explained adequately to the rational mind, because when we are dealing with things that are spiritual and supernatural – beyond reason. The thoughts of God are much higher than our thoughts.

To believe something that is opposed to the revelation of the Bible is, therefore, deception. People can be deceived by having false ideas about Jesus or the nature of God. The problem is that a person is only deceived when he or she wrongly thinks he's right!

It is common to hear people say: "I have my own ideas about God." That can be a quick way to hell. It is to create one's own "god."

The only way to salvation is through the one true God. Everyone has to submit his own thoughts, ideas and opinions to the revelation of truth in the New Testament. We are most certainly deceived if we believe we have some greater or even different revelation other than the truth revealed by Jesus.

Jesus said:

"Whoever belongs to God hears what God says."

(John 8:47)

Nobody can think his own way to God, or do anything to make himself acceptable to him. It is deception to believe that there could be any other way to have a relationship with God than through Jesus Christ, for God has chosen to reveal himself through his Son.

This sounds dogmatic, and it is! When it comes to the truth, the Christian has to be dogmatic. For the truth is not a matter of debate but of revelation through Jesus, the Word of God. We want to reveal the truth to others in love but we cannot compromise that truth. The New Testament contains many warnings to the believers in Jesus Christ not to be deceived by departing from the revelation of truth.

Within the scope of this booklet, it is impossible to describe all the Bible reveals about the truth. You will have to turn to the Bible itself for that. We can only consider some of the warnings the scriptures give us about deception.

2

The deceiver

Satan is the deceiver. He *"leads the whole world astray"* (Revelation 12:9). He is the god of this age who *"has blinded the minds of unbelievers, so that they cannot see the light of the gospel of the glory of Christ, who is the image of God"* (2 Corinthians 4:4).

Satan wants to encourage sin and lawlessness so that people will remain under judgment and condemnation, rather than receive the salvation made possible through faith in Jesus Christ. He wants them to suppress the truth.

> *The wrath of God is being revealed from heaven against all the godlessness and wickedness of those who suppress the truth by their wickedness, since what may be known about God is plain to them, because God has made it plain to them. For since the creation of the world God's invisible qualities – his eternal power and divine nature – have been clearly seen, being understood from what has been made, so that they are without excuse.*
>
> (Romans 1:18–20)

The enemy does not want people to acknowledge the obvious evidence all around them of the existence of a creator God. For two reasons, he does not want us to submit ourselves to God's authority.

First, Satan himself is in rebellion against God. Therefore he encourages rebellion in the world; he wants to deceive nations (Revelation 20:8).

Second, he knows that when a person submits to God's authority, this gives the believer power over the enemy. Jesus said:

> *"I saw Satan fall like lightning from heaven. I have given you authority to trample on snakes and scorpions, and to overcome all the power of the enemy; nothing will harm you."*
>
> (Luke 10:18–19)

Because of this, Satan will do everything he can to prevent a person coming into a relationship of faith in Jesus. He makes his appeal to the flesh, encouraging people to believe that they will only receive satisfaction and personal fulfillment through material prosperity, sexual promiscuity and other forms of self-indulgence.

The more people indulge themselves in these fleshly pursuits the more they crave for those things that are sinful in God's sight. They discover ultimately that none of these pursuits lead to the true happiness they seek.

Satan's ultimate purpose is to destroy people. He will destroy them spiritually by encouraging them not to believe in God, to deny there is a spiritual dimension to life. Jesus warned:

> *"The thief comes only to steal and kill and destroy."*
>
> (John 10:10)

By contrast, Jesus comes to give life, God's life in abundance!

Satan will even try to destroy a person physically. He encourages suicide, sickness and even so-called accidents. Because he knows that only the truth will set people free, the devil encourages counterfeit religions and cults. If people must believe in a god, he would have them believe in what is false, because a false god cannot rescue anyone from Satan's grasp.

The counterfeit

▶ *The devil tries to counterfeit the real thing in order to deceive.*
Healings can be attributed to spiritualists, but people are put into bondage by the spirits that are invoked. I have even had to deliver in the name of Jesus two spiritualists renowned for their "healings." They were in fact in bondage themselves to the demonic spirits they had used.

Supernatural events certainly take place through the occult. People in Christian ministry will testify to having to deliver many who have dabbled with ouija boards, various forms of fortune-telling and even some computer games, things the unwary consider harmless.

▶ *The enemy appeals to the flesh in order to deceive people.*
He appears as an angel of light. Often people cannot see that something that appears good can lead them into bondage.

Freemasonry is a prime example. It appears good because of the caring work it supports. And although it is officially denied, many are attracted by the financial and social advantages to belonging to such a brotherhood. People become masons because they expect to benefit in their business and social life as a result.

Many try to dismiss the fact that masons pray to false gods and take binding oaths to them. This is the height of deception. You will not find liberty in the Holy Spirit in the lives of church-going Freemasons; neither will there be such liberty in congregations where Freemasons are in positions of leadership or control.

▶ *Deception can never lead to freedom.*
The counterfeit may have some appeal but it inevitably leaves the person in bondage. Instead of encouraging people to be responsible disciples, it encourages them to excuse their sin and disobedience. Often there is the suggestion that a person cannot exercise faith or enjoy the new life given in Jesus because of previous rejection and hurts.

Such teaching denies the truth that the old has gone, crucified with Christ. The new has come and the believer can enjoy his rich inheritance with Christ through faith.

The enemy will try to counterfeit the gifts of the Holy Spirit. He will attempt sometimes to disrupt the course of a meeting with false prophecy. He will inspire false messages in order to lead believers astray, often appealing to our pride. That is why we should test everything.

▶   *No believer should take significant decisions for their life purely on the basis of a "word" given to them by somebody else.*

Each believer is to hear God for himself or herself. The Lord will often confirm what he is saying through other witnesses, but they are not to replace the voice of the Lord directly to the believer. So it is important for every Christian to spend time waiting on God, listening to him and being humble enough to test what has been heard against Bible revelation. Christians also need to accept correction from God or other people, if their views have diverged from the truth.

The devil will try to prevent people from using the spiritual gifts by suggesting that they are not real. He knows how powerful these gifts are and it is in his interest to prevent their use. Many believers have been deceived by his accusation that their "tongue," the language given by the Holy Spirit, is not real. They are also hindered from bringing interpretations or prophecies because of the suggestion that they may be wrong.

The enemy incites church leaders not to allow spiritual gifts in public worship, directly opposing the instructions of scripture (1 Corinthians 14:26–40). He instills a spirit of fear to try and counteract the spirit of faith that is meant to operate in every Christian (2 Corinthians 4:13).

We need the Holy Spirit to bring prophetic revelation both personally and corporately. There is no need to fear going wrong or being deceived if we are prepared to test everything against the truth. It is only when people court deception by actually preferring to believe something other than the truth, that problems arise.

3

Other religions and cults

Only the truth of Jesus Christ will set people free from sin, judgment and condemnation. Only faith in Jesus will free them from the devil's grasp. To believe something other than the truth will leave people in bondage. This is the sad reality for many who are part of other religions and cults.

Before we look at these we must bear one uncomfortable aspect of the truth in mind. No man, no matter how religious, devout or sincere he may be, has any claim on God. Because all have sinned and fall short of God's glory (Romans 3:23), we cannot please God through our natural abilities.

Jesus made it clear:

> *"Apart from me you can do nothing."*   (John 15:5)

Whatever we do apart from Jesus is worthless. He is our means of acceptance by the Father. He is perfectly just in his judgment on sin and the sinner, and yet because he loves us, he doesn't desire to condemn but to save. That is why God provided Jesus to be the way of salvation.

> *"For God so loved the world that he gave his one and only Son, that whoever believes in him shall not perish but have eternal life. For God did not send his Son into the world to condemn the world, but to save the world through him. Those who believe in him are not condemned, but those who do not believe stand*

condemned already because they have not believed in the name of God's one and only Son." (John 3:16–18)

We cannot escape the fact that all other religions and cults are false; they come out of deception. They give people the impression that they are valid ways to know God, whereas in fact they cannot offer a relationship of love with God as Father now, they cannot free a person from sin and death, nor can they give to anyone the gift of eternal life.

Jesus said:

"I tell you the truth, those who hear my word and believe him who sent me have eternal life and will not be condemned; they have crossed over from death to life." (John 5:24)

No religion can even claim to give people such a relationship, eternal life and God's kingdom *now!*

Jesus did not come to establish another religion; nothing could have been further from his desires. He came with the gift of God's life:

"I have come that they may have life, and have it to the full." (John 10:10)

He came to make it possible for us to belong to God's kingdom and to be empowered to live the life of that kingdom on earth. He wants us to enjoy a personal relationship with him so that we can fulfill his purposes.

It is not the intention of Christians to stand in judgment on those who belong to other religions and cults. We want to reach out to them with the truth. However, because of the nature of deception (people believing they are right when they are not) it is common for those of other beliefs to reject the Christian gospel, the very means of delivering them from their deception.

The devil opposes the truth. His initial approach to Eve in the garden of Eden was to question what God had said. Satan wants people to be deceived and so miss the way of salvation. God did not send his Son to be one of the many ways of salvation. If it was possible for salvation to be obtained in any other way, he certainly would not have humbled himself by becoming a man, suffering constant persecution and rejection by those he came to save, and then dying an agonizing death on the cross for them! Jesus subjected himself to all these indignities because he knew this to be the only way that sinful people could be reconciled with God.

Some of the false religions and cults claim to believe in Jesus. But they do not believe what the New Testament reveals about him: that he is God, he is Lord, the truth, the only Savior. They reduce him to only a prophet, a good teacher, one among many gods, a spiritual force among many spirits to which you can pray.

This is the main way to test whether a group of people belong to the truth or not: what do they believe about the person of Jesus? If they do not accept that he is God and Lord, they do not belong to the truth. Sadly, they are deceived.

It is impossible to give a summary of world religions and cults. Below are a few examples to show how people can be deceived because of their misconceptions of Christ. We will begin with Judaism, the faith of the Jews into which Jesus was born.

The Jewish faith

God first revealed his purposes and made a covenant with his chosen people through Abraham. The Old Testament is all about his dealings with the Jewish people. In its earliest years, the Church was almost entirely Jewish and was at first regarded as an offshoot of Judaism.

At the time of Christ, people could not account for the mighty miracles he performed, and many Jews acknowledged that no one taught with such authority as Jesus. Yet a large number rejected him, and the rejection of that generation has been passed on to subsequent generations.

It is tragic that any of the Jews should reject their own Messiah. They worship his Father as God, and yet reject Jesus as his Son. Instead of believing in him, the religious leaders of his day wanted him put to death! To him he was an imposter who made false claims.

The New Testament is clear that God has allowed a veil to be drawn over the Jewish understanding of Jesus so that the harvest of the Gentile believers can be gathered. Before Jesus returns, there will be a significant move of God among the Jewish people who will then accept Jesus for who he truly is, their Messiah.

The Gospel is the same for all:

> *For there is no difference between Jew and Gentile – the same Lord is Lord of all and richly blesses all who call on him, for, "Everyone who calls on the name of the Lord will be saved."*
>
> (Romans 10:12–13)

The law God gave to the Jews informed them of what he desired of his people, but could not give them the power to obey. Nobody is able to keep the law perfectly. All of us sin, and *"therefore no one will be declared righteous in his sight by observing the law; rather, through the law we become conscious of sin"* (Romans 3:20).

God had to give the law first to prove to people that, no matter how hard they tried in their own strength, it was impossible to succeed in pleasing God by their own efforts or works. Salvation is a work of God's grace; it is a gift received from him in response to the faith placed in Jesus.

> *This righteousness from God comes through faith in Jesus Christ to all who believe.*   (Romans 3:22)

People can only be justified, made totally acceptable in God's sight, through his grace. Paul, himself brought up to be a very strictly religious Jew, went to great lengths to make clear to his Jewish brethren that no one can be saved through trying to keep the law.

This is a message of great relevance for many church-going people today, for they have substituted the Jewish law with a Christian "law," denominational rules. They believe falsely they can please God by going to church and diligently observing their religious duties. This is also deception. Our acceptance depends entirely on faith in what Jesus has done for us. The writer to the Hebrews quotes Jeremiah 31 in prophesying:

The time is coming, declares the Lord,
  when I will make a new covenant
with the house of Israel
  and with the house of Judah.
It will not be like the covenant
  I made with their ancestors
when I took them by the hand
  to lead them out of Egypt,
because they did not remain faithful to my covenant,
  and I turned away from them,
                                               declares the Lord.
This is the covenant I will make with the house of Israel
  after that time, declares the Lord.
I will put my laws in their minds
  and write them on their hearts.
I will be their God,
  and they will be my people.   (Hebrews 8:8–10)

No Christian should forget his Jewish roots. We should all pray and long for the harvest of God's kingdom among the Jewish people. God's promises to them will surely be fulfilled.

Islam

"There is no god but Allah, and Mohammed is the Messenger of God." This is the Muslim's confession of faith and is in direct conflict with the truth of Jesus Christ.

"Allah" is in reality a deceiving spirit. Mohammed, who was

rejected from becoming a Christian minister, started his own religion with devastating consequences. The strength of Islam today is evidence of how rapidly deception can spread and what a total grip it can have on a person's life.

The Koran is the sacred book of Islam and believed by Muslims to be the absolute word of God. They profess belief in the Old and New Testaments, but the Koran is regarded as God's final revelation. Anything in the Bible that disagrees with the Koran is considered to have been corrupted by human beings or divinely superseded in the Koran.

The Trinity is scorned as Muslims believe that God is one, and that faith in Jesus Christ as God is blasphemy. Islam accepts the virgin birth and the scriptural accounts of the miracles of Jesus, but see him as a prophet and teacher, not God's Son. Because they do not believe in the doctrine of original sin, a savior is not required. Salvation is by good deeds and devotion to God – a Muslim's destiny in the next life is determined by his works.

The word *Islam* means "surrender" and submission to the will of God is the way of salvation. So for example if you are poor, this is considered God's will – "So be it." This is a form of fatalism, accepting that everything that happens to you must be God's will. It is very different from Jesus' encouragement to pray with faith, believing that God will answer by changing circumstances.

Jehovah's Witnesses

It is sad that followers of many false religions and cults show a fervor and enthusiasm for their faith that puts many Christians to shame. Jehovah's Witnesses are an example of this. They are extremely zealous and sincere people who claim to accept the Bible as their only authority. In reality they constantly misuse scripture to establish their own beliefs.

The official publication of Jehovah's Witnesses, *The Watchtower* magazine, is considered the voice that speaks God's word to the world. The teaching propagated through the magazine actually takes precedence over the scriptures, even though *The Watchtower* contends that the scriptures are their final authority. Biblical texts are deliberately mistranslated from the original Greek and changed to suit JW teaching in what they call the "New World Translation."

Renowned for their door-to-door techniques, Jehovah's Witnesses deceive by posing as Christians or by suggesting "we believe the same things." They have been notorious for their refusal to allow blood transfusions in medical emergencies and are very defensive when challenged about their belief that only 144,000 will go to heaven.

Jehovah's Witnesses deny the divinity of Jesus Christ and believe him to be a created being – a god with a small "g." They do not believe that the death of Christ atones for our sin, and neither do they believe in his bodily resurrection. They believe salvation is by works, not by grace through faith, and they deny the existence of hell as a place of everlasting punishment.

Mormonism

Mormonism – founded by a man in response to two visions – has several different sources of authority: the Bible, the *Book of Mormon*, the *Doctrine and Covenants* and *The Pearl of Great Price*. The Mormon church claims that it is God's only restored, true church on earth, whilst all others are wrong.

Mormons say, "We believe the Bible to be the word of God in so far as it is translated correctly." However, they put more trust in the other three books than the Bible, as they claim the scriptures have been corrupted and changed throughout the centuries. They also believe that the prophets (Mormon church leaders) living today speak words more vital than the written words. "When our leaders think, the thinking has been done – when they propose a plan, it is God's plan."

Mormons give the impression that they believe the doctrine of the Trinity, but this is not so. They believe in many gods and that God himself was once a man. Mormon males are considered to have the potential of becoming gods themselves.

Mormons view Jesus as *a* Son of God, not as *the* Son of God. He is considered "the older brother" and through his atonement mankind is saved by obedience to the laws. There is no eternal punishment and the level of individual salvation is based on obedience to the Mormon teaching.

New Age movements

All kinds of New Age teaching have become fashionable in recent years, but there is nothing new about it. Because this teaching covers such a wide range of ideas it is difficult to be concise.

Many followers of New Age teaching deny the divinity of Jesus Christ or the Trinity. They deny the work of Jesus' death on the cross to deliver us from sin, and also the reality of sin and death, heaven and hell. Some church people embrace New Age teaching, ignorant of the fact that it is basically humanism overlaid with a pagan spirituality.

Most New Age thinking has strong links with Hinduism in believing that "God is all and all is God." Followers often worship their own being through meditation, yoga, witchcraft and occult practices. They believe that human beings contain their own capacity for salvation and have the potential of becoming gods through reaching a higher consciousness.

New Age teaching is appealing because it advocates world peace, racial harmony, feminism and ecumenical inter-faith programs. Adherents speak of a new world order, but see this as being brought about by a system of political control. They seek a messiah, not Jesus but the one the scriptures warn against, the deceiver who wants to exercise dominion over the earth.

Common factors

There are a number of common factors in this small selection of religions and cults.

1. They do not believe in the divinity of Jesus Christ.

2. They do not believe in the Trinity: God as Father, Son and Holy Spirit.

3. Salvation is through human efforts toward self-improvement or through obedience to law. It is not understood as a gracious gift from God, received only through faith in Jesus Christ.

4. They do not accept the New Testament as a unique revelation of divine truth. They either add to it from other sources regarded as equally or more authentic, or subtract or deny some aspects of Jesus' teaching. Others change the scriptures to suit their own beliefs.

Inter-faith services

Inter-faith services are becoming popular in some places, yet they are clearly deceptive, because they involve worshiping together with those who oppose faith in the true God revealed in Jesus Christ. The biblical name for this is idolatry. Israel was constantly warned of the calamities that would befall the nation for indulging in such practices.

All religions which oppose the truth must be demonically inspired. Paul makes clear:

You cannot drink the cup of the Lord and demons too.
(1 Corinthians 10:21)

It is claimed that partaking in inter-faith services is an act of love and outreach. Yet do we really love people by giving the impression that we are happy to pray with them while they are worshiping false spirits? Surely the only true way to love them is to stand up for the truth: that no one can come to the Father except by Jesus!

In a multi-faith context it is impossible to claim that Jesus gives the only true revelation of God because he is himself God. We would compromise that claim by suggesting the Christian faith is just one of several ways to God. To do so would certainly be taking part in deception.

4

Warnings to Christians

Deception is one of the basic ways in which the devil will attack Christians. He tries to lead us away from faith in God's word, for he knows that such faith defeats evil.

The enemy encourages Christians to doubt what God has done for them. He tries to deceive them into thinking that the revelation of scripture cannot be true, that God will not keep his promises.

The devil is the accuser of our brothers and sisters (Revelation 12:10). He suggests to unwary Christians that if God truly loved us, we would not face problems. By trying to make us feel condemned, he undermines confidence in our salvation. He plants negative thoughts, desires and actions, and then blames the believer for having them, suggesting that we are no longer acceptable to God.

He is the father of lies, and it is his nature to lie and deceive people. Therefore every Christian needs to have a good grasp of the truth of God's word, otherwise he will not know how to withstand the enemy's attacks. When tempted in the wilderness, Jesus responded by saying to Satan:

> "It is written: People do not live on bread alone, but on every word that comes from the mouth of God."   (Matthew 4:4)

That is how we should respond, too. The enemy knows the

scriptures and will try to deceive us by misquoting them to us, or by taking things out of context and twisting their meaning. The devil will try to deceive us by placing negative, unbelieving thoughts in our minds. He may try to do this directly or through others, even other Christians. Peter learned to his cost that he could be a mouthpiece of Satan as well as of God (Matthew 16:23). The enemy is able to appear as an angel of light (2 Corinthians 11:14), so we have to beware false teachers who would attempt to deceive even God's chosen ones.

We too can be Satan's mouthpiece if we say things about ourselves and others that are untrue, a denial of what God says in his word. The enemy understands the power over us of the words we speak, and that our tongues are like ships' rudders steering the course of our lives (James 3:4–5). He wants to steer us off course instead of being true to what God says to us.

Scripture tells us that as born-again believers we are accepted as children of God (John 1:12–13), we are made righteous and holy in God's sight (Ephesians 1:4, Colossians 1:22), that nothing in all creation can separate us from God's love (Romans 8:35), and that he always leads us in his triumphal procession in Christ (2 Corinthians 2:14). We have the shield of faith with which we are able to extinguish all the flaming arrows of the evil one (Ephesians 6:16)!

Jesus encourages us to ask, seek and knock (Matthew 7:7–8). But Satan suggests that God will not listen to us, that he would not want to heal us or perform miracles in our lives. Satan wants to deceive us into thinking that we are no-good, useless failures, and that God could not possibly want anything to do with us.

The devil cannot take away the salvation and inheritance God has given a born-again Christian. He cannot take the Holy Spirit away from us. But he will continue to try to divert believers from the truth so that we will not enjoy the *"glorious freedom of the children of God"* (Romans 8:21) or be able to exercise Jesus' authority against him. He wants to keep us on the defensive so we do not plunder his territory, rescuing others from sin, condemnation and death.

Faith is a choice and we have to decide whether we are going to believe the truth or listen to the deceiver. Satan's tactics are to undermine your faith in God's word and in what Jesus has done for you. When he deceived Eve, he provoked doubt in God's truthfulness and her ability to hear and understand his word:

> *The serpent was more crafty than any of the wild animals the* LORD *God had made. He said to the woman, "Did God really say, 'You must not eat from any tree in the garden'?"*
>
> *The woman said to the serpent, "We may eat fruit from the trees in the garden, but God did say, 'You must not eat fruit from the tree that is in the middle of the garden, and you must not touch it, or you will die.' "*
>
> *"You will not surely die," the serpent said to the woman. "For God knows that when you eat of it your eyes will be opened, and you will be like God, knowing good and evil."* (Genesis 3:1–5)

Having succeeded in causing Eve to question God's word, the serpent then directly contradicted what God had said. He does the same today. He tempts people to question the word of God to them, undermines their faith, and leads them to contradict God's word in what they do and say.

False doctrine

Even within churches which call themselves Christian, there is a great diversity of doctrine and practice. For the most part, these differences relate to non-essential matters. The main tenets of the Christian faith have been incorporated in the historic creeds that have been passed on from generation to generation of believers.

The creeds were written to counteract heresies in the early centuries of the Church's history. As statements of faith, they briefly encapsulate the main truths, but are by no means exhaustive. Only the scriptures can be the full standard of truth.

Many of the deceptive doctrines taught by some who call themselves Christians (even by some bishops and denominational leaders) are not new. They are the old heresies put in modern language and relate especially to the nature of Jesus. For example, some deny the virgin birth, even though this is the clear revelation of scripture. By doing so, they refuse to believe that Jesus was conceived by the Holy Spirit and therefore had a divine nature in his humanity. Some have tried to make Jesus less than God, while both the Bible and the creeds make clear the trinity of Father, Son and Holy Spirit.

Others have suggested that Jesus did not truly die on the cross. If this was the case, there would be no adequate sacrifice for our sins, since no sacrifice would actually have been made. It is important that we understand that Jesus was crucified, dead and buried! And he rose from the dead, having overcome death and hell in the process.

Some have supported the view that Jesus was not physically raised from the dead, that his body was stolen by his disciples to suggest that he had been raised. Paul points out:

> *And if Christ has not been raised, your faith is futile; you are still in your sins. Then those also who have fallen asleep in Christ are lost. If only for this life we have hope in Christ, we are to be pitied more than all people.*   (1 Corinthians 15:17–19)

Still others suggest that there is no bodily resurrection, which again denies the revelation of scripture. Jesus had a risen body which was the same, and yet different, from his physical body. The same is true for those who believe in him. Paul taught:

> *So will it be with the resurrection of the dead. The body that is sown is perishable, it is raised imperishable; it is sown in dishonor, it is raised in glory; it is sown in weakness, it is raised in power.*   (1 Corinthians 15:42–43)

Those who question the truth of scriptural revelation do so out of pride. They raise their intellect above the truth revealed by God. They are confused and those who listen join them in their confusion.

▶ *All deception ultimately leads to confusion.*

We all find things in the New Testament that are hard to understand or to find a rational explanation for. However, our lack of understanding does not invalidate the truth. As we choose to believe what we read, we discover that the Holy Spirit will open up our understanding.

I understand much more of the scriptures now than when I first became a Christian over 40 years ago. However, the truth has always been the truth, long before I discovered it as such! There are still things in the Bible I do not understand. But I believe them and know that the Holy Spirit will give me revelation of other truths in due course.

God certainly will not change his word for you, me or anyone else!

▶ *The truth is the truth and is eternal; it can never change.*

Jesus said:

"Heaven and earth will pass away; but my words will never pass away." (Matthew 24:35)

True and false counseling

Jesus makes it clear that the truth will set people free. It is important, therefore, that when people seek counsel they receive the truth as taught in the scriptures, rather than human ideas and opinions. The truth points us to the completed work that Jesus has accomplished to meet every need in our lives.

The ministry of counselor in the New Testament belongs to Jesus and the Holy Spirit. Jesus promised that the Holy Spirit, the Spirit of truth, would guide us into all the truth. If you do not believe what God's word says about you, then you do not believe the truth. And when you believe something other than the truth, you are deceived.

Some counseling and deliverance ministries with a non-biblical emphasis have emerged in the Church today. Such ministries often encourage people to look to others for help rather than look directly to the Lord.

There is one mediator between God and human beings, Jesus Christ. He came to make it possible for every believer to have a personal relationship with him. He says to all who are weary or burdened: *"Come to me"* (Matthew 11:28).

Sometimes people will need to be helped to come to Jesus. Those who receive such help, however, need to be taught to depend on Jesus, not on the one seeking to help them.

Paul states clearly: *"I have been crucified with Christ and I no longer live, but Christ lives in me"* (Galatians 2:20). This indicates that the people we were before we were born again are no longer alive.

> *We were buried with him through baptism into death in order that, just as Christ was raised from the dead through the glory of the Father, we too may live a new life.*   (Romans 6:4)

Now we are new creations. The new life can only be lived by faith, the faith that believes that God loves me and gave himself for me. Paul said:

> *The life I live in the body, I live by faith in the Son of God, who loved me and gave himself for me.*   (Galatians 2:20)

Every one of my needs has therefore been met by what he did on the cross. What do we all want to experience in this life? Love, joy, peace, patience, kindness, goodness, gentleness, faithfulness and self-control! These are the fruit of the Spirit that God has available for the believer (Galatians 5:22), and should be what we aim for in ourselves and in others.

By the sacrifice of Jesus *"we have been made holy"* (Hebrews 10:10) and *"made perfect forever"* (verse 14). Yet as believers we do not manifest that holiness and perfection completely in our soul life. To some measure we reflect the Lord's glory, but we *"are being transformed in his likeness with ever-increasing glory, which comes from the Lord, who is the Spirit"* (2 Corinthians 3:18). Paul later affirms: *"It is for freedom that Christ has set us free"* (Galatians 5:1). He has already done it! We are called to live by faith in what he has done. Some people become even more discouraged as they look at themselves and center their thoughts on who they once were, instead of who they now are. It is important that counseling does not increase a sense of bondage to the past.

This transformation of character comes from the Holy Spirit. Only he can make us like Jesus. Self-analysis cannot in itself bring about the healing and wholeness we desire. Three things hinder the process of becoming like Christ:

1. *Unbelief*: Instead of putting faith in what Jesus has said and done, we choose to believe something else about ourselves.

2. *Unforgiveness*: We remain bound to people who have hurt, abused, rejected or opposed us until we forgive them. Jesus was very forthright about this: if we do not forgive others, God will not forgive us. We will have no sense of personal freedom or victory unless we know we are forgiven.

3. *Disobedience*: We hear the word but do not do it.

Some protest that they are unable to believe, forgive and obey. Yet this is not true for any Christian, for each of these three things is an act of the will, and God has given each of us freedom of choice.

It is the responsibility to every believer to submit to God and resist the devil until he flees (James 4:7). We have to resist the enemy ourselves, not expect someone to do it for us.

We each choose what to believe: what God says, or what opposes what he says. No one can do our believing for us. We choose to forgive or not to forgive; forgiveness is a choice, not an emotion. No one can forgive on our behalf. We also choose to obey God's word, because no one else can obey on our behalf.

Those counseling in the power of the Holy Spirit will encourage people to believe, forgive and obey. They will not take the responsibility away from the believer to do the things he or she is to do for himself or herself.

God's word works for every believer. It is the devil's deception to suggest otherwise, and to discourage faith in what Jesus has done.

5

Unbelief

▶ *When we do not believe what Jesus said, we must believe
something else instead!*
In other words, to disagree with the truth is to believe something that is false and therefore deceptive.

Everything Jesus said was the truth. But sometimes he
prefaced his remarks with the phrase *"Truly, truly"* or, *"I tell
you the truth."* He not only used this phrase to stress that what
he was about to say was of great importance, but because he
knew his words would be met with unbelief by his listeners.
They might find it difficult to believe, but nevertheless what he
was about to say is the truth.

We can only look at a few examples here. Yet from this
selection you can see that it is very tempting to try and explain
away what Jesus says, so that you do not have to apply it to
yourself.

*"I tell you the truth, if you have faith and do not doubt, not only
can you do what was done to the fig tree, but also you can say to
this mountain, 'Go, throw yourself into the sea', and it will be
done. If you believe, you will receive whatever you ask for in
prayer."*   (Matthew 21:21–22)

*"I tell you the truth, all who have faith in me will do what I have
been doing, and they will do even greater things than these,
because I am going to the Father."*   (John 14:12)

*"If anyone comes to me and does not hate father and mother,
wife and children, brothers and sisters – yes, even life itself –
such a person cannot be my disciple. And those who do not carry
their cross and follow me cannot be my disciples."*

(Luke 14:26–27)

Such sayings of Jesus are a challenge to both our faith and our
commitment to him. *God wants to bring our thinking into line with
his thinking!*

Often we are guilty of unbelief through a lack of understanding. For example, at first sight it seems blasphemous to suggest
that the believer can do greater things than Jesus. Yet this is
what he clearly says. What does he mean? The clue is in the
phrase *"because I am going to the Father."*

What happened when Jesus went to the Father? God fulfilled
his promise to send the Holy Spirit to those who believe in
Jesus. This meant that they could then pray for others to be
filled with the Holy Spirit, something Jesus did not do because
during his earthly ministry the Holy Spirit had not yet been
poured out:

> *By this he meant the Spirit, whom those who believed in him
> were later to receive. Up to that time the Spirit had not been
> given, since Jesus had not yet been glorified.*   (John 7:39)

When you realize that you can pray for others and the Holy
Spirit will come upon them, then you see that it is God's
purpose for believers to do greater works than Jesus! This does
not become the truth because you believe it. It has always been
the truth. When you choose to believe it you can act upon it,
impossible though it may seem!

Experience can be another enemy of the truth. You may well
have asked for many things in prayer which you have not
received, and genuinely believed you prayed with faith. So how
can it be right to say as Jesus does that *"if you believe, you will
receive whatever you ask for in prayer"*?

In such situations you are to choose who is right: God or you. Is Jesus the truth, or is your experience the truth? Will God change his word to bring it in line with your experience? Or does he want to bring your experience into line with his word of truth? Is not God's estimate of the situation more accurate than your own? After all, he knows every thought, desire, motive and intention. He knows whether you believed you had already received the answer and were thanking him for what he had done; or whether you were still just *hoping* that he would do something about your problem.

▶ *It is deception to imagine that we have a better grasp of any situation than God!*
We have to bow before his greater wisdom and understanding. We have to accept that he always acts in righteousness and truth. He will never deceive his children, neither will he fail to honor the faith that is put in him.

▶ *It is also deception to imagine that God is happy for you to choose the level of discipleship that is acceptable to you.*
Doing so waters down what Jesus teaches. He makes it clear that love for him must come before all else, including love for father and mother, wife and children, even love of self. The disciple is to hate the very idea of anyone or anything coming before God in his priorities.
To give God his rightful place will bring blessing not only to us as disciples, but also to those we love, especially those closest to us.

▶ *It is deception to hear what God says and not to put it into operation* (Matthew 7:24)
If we hear the word and fail to put it into practice, we are like a man building his house on sand. When the storms came, his house fell. Jesus likens the one who obeys the word to the man who built his house on rock. The house withstood the storm.

You will often find that a Christian is struggling when confronted with a problem because he is not being obedient to the Lord. He is seeking to pray with faith and does not necessarily see that the area of disobedience has anything to do with an entirely unrelated problem.

We are deceived when we imagine that our life is divided into air-tight compartments. God weighs the heart and knows everything in every believer's life. Sometimes he allows difficult circumstances to encourage us to face areas of disobedience, or our need to trust more wholeheartedly in his words and promises.

We set ourselves up against God when we disagree with him. David said:

> *Surely you desire truth in the inner parts;*
> *you teach me wisdom in the inmost place.*   (Psalm 51:6)

He is the one who is above all, and yet he dwells with those who are of a *"humble and contrite heart"* (Psalm 51:17). We are not truly humble before God unless we submit ourselves to his word. Failure to do this will inevitably lead to deception.

False teachers

The apostle John wrote: *"I have no greater joy than to hear that my children are walking in the truth"* (3 John 4). He wrote to those *"whom I love in the truth"* (3 John 1). He says the truth lives in us and will be with us forever (2 John 2). But he warns his readers to beware of false teachers.

> *Many deceivers, who do not acknowledge Jesus Christ as coming in the flesh, have gone out into the world. Any such person is the deceiver and the antichrist. Watch out that you do not lose what you have worked for, but that you may be rewarded fully. Anyone who runs ahead and does not continue in the teaching*

of Christ does not have God; whoever continues in the teaching has both the Father and the Son. (2 John 7–9)

This is indeed a grave warning. Even in New Testament times there were many false teachers. The same heresies they taught – such as denying the true humanity of Jesus – are around today.

Some are the legalists who prefer their own religious law to God's grace:

For there are many rebellious people, mere talkers and deceivers, especially those of the circumcision group. They must be silenced, because they are ruining whole households by teaching things they ought not to teach – and that for the sake of dishonest gain. (Titus 1:10–11)

Paul also speaks of *"false apostles, deceitful workers, masquerading as apostles of Christ"* (2 Corinthians 11:13). They *"preach a Jesus other than the Jesus we preached"* (that is, the Jesus of the New Testament), come in a different spirit, and bring a different gospel (2 Corinthians 11:4).

False teachers try to take people captive *"through hollow and deceptive philosophy, which depends on human traditions and the basic principles of this world rather than on Christ"* (Colossians 2:8). These are the ones who exalt reason and traditions above God's word. They suggest that you are free to think, believe and do what you think best without any reference to the revelation of divine truth.

Jesus also warned people to *"beware of the teachers of the law"* (Luke 20:46). They were the ones who were full of self-importance, who loved recognition and showed off by saying lengthy prayers. But they opposed the gospel of God's grace. They were not motivated by love of the truth or love for people, but only by their self-love.

Paul looked forward to the day when the body of Christ was built up to the extent that *"we all reach unity in the faith and in*

the knowledge of the Son of God and become mature, attaining to the whole measure of the fullness of Christ" (Ephesians 4:13).
He went on,

> *Then we will no longer be infants, tossed back and forth by the waves, and blown here and there by every wind of teaching and by the cunning and craftiness of people in their deceitful scheming. Instead, speaking the truth in love, we will in all things grow up into him who is the head, that is, Christ.*
>
> (Ephesians 4:14–15)

False prophets

We are warned about false prophets as well as false teachers. Jeremiah complained, *"prophets and priests alike, all practice deceit"* (Jeremiah 6:13).

> *The Spirit clearly says that in later times some will abandon the faith and follow deceiving spirits and things taught by demons.*
>
> (1 Timothy 4:1)

The deceiver uses spirits to try and seduce people away from the truth. For this reason John warned:

> *Dear friends, do not believe every spirit, but test the spirits to see whether they are from God, because many false prophets have gone out into the world. This is how you can recognize the Spirit of God: Every spirit that acknowledges that Jesus Christ has come in the flesh is from God, but every spirit that does not acknowledge Jesus is not from God. This is the spirit of the antichrist, which you have heard is coming and even now is already in the world.*   (1 John 4:1–3)

Notice how John emphasized that *the test of what is true or false hinges on whether these prophets agree with the biblical revelation of Jesus.*

Prophecy is God speaking to his people. So it is deceptive when someone claims to speak from God, but is either giving Satan's words or speaks from his or her own mind. For this reason, we are urged to test every prophecy to see whether it is of God. The final test of prophecy is to see whether what is said agrees with the truth, with God's word.

The Holy Spirit would not inspire anyone to speak against the revelation of truth. His purpose is to lead people into the truth. Jesus teaches us that even the Holy Spirit does not speak independently from the Father. He speaks only what he hears. God's Spirit does not deny his word but instead reveals it to the believer.

Opposition to the truth

There will always be those inspired by demonic spirits who deliberately oppose the truth. Paul and Barnabas had an encounter with Elymas the sorcerer. Paul said to him:

> *You are a child of the devil and an enemy of everything that is right! You are full of all kinds of deceit and trickery. Will you never stop perverting all the right ways of the Lord?*
>
> (Acts 13:10)

The allure of the occult is that it offers people power or knowledge while putting those in bondage to the deceiving spirits that are involved in occult activity. This includes such activities as black magic, witchcraft, clairvoyance, fortune-telling, palm-reading, divining, yoga, freemasonry, and some forms of alternative medicine, including healing through spiritism.

Christians should not only avoid such activities like the plague, but renounce completely any previous involvement in the occult. We need to stand against any deceiving spirits that could have influenced our life.

Any ties with the occult that have come down the generations, such as masonic vows or connections to spiritism through ancestors, must be cut. If we have any charms, literature or other articles related to involvement in the occult or foreign gods, they must be destroyed. We also have to give up any superstitious practices. God is not superstitious!

6

Causes of deception

Certain things aid the enemy in his attempts to deceive you. There can be ways in which you tend to deceive yourself, or to prefer a half-truth, because you do not want to face up to the demands of faith. When this is the case, Satan will make the most of the opportunity you give him through your unbelief or disobedience.

The enemy appeals to the flesh, encouraging us to exalt reason above the truth of God's word, to prefer doubt to faith, to hold onto tradition rather than the truth, to believe the circumstances rather than God's promises.

The Bible says we can be either deceived or self-deceived in a number of ways. Every Christian needs to test his heart and life against the truths of scripture.

Pride

Pride prefers self to God or anyone else. Whatever opposes God must be the work of deception.

One of the prophets wrote:

> *The pride of your heart has deceived you.* (Obadiah 3)

God opposes the proud; he brings them down. But he lifts up and gives grace to the humble.

41

Humble yourselves, therefore, under God's mighty hand, that he may lift you up in due time.   (1 Peter 5:6)

When we are proud and conceited, we are *blind to our own sin and weakness.*

John tells us:

If we claim to be without sin, we deceive ourselves and the truth is not in us.   (1 John 1:8)

None of us has yet reached the stage of perfection. Our thinking is imperfect, our prophecy is imperfect, and we do not yet walk in total surrender or obedience. Every Christian must remember this and beware of self-righteousness.

False ideas about ourselves are another form of self-deception.

If any of you think you are something when you are nothing, you deceive yourselves.   (Galatians 6:3)

Paul goes on to say that each of us should test our own actions, not comparing ourselves with others but receiving instruction from the word.

Self-dependence

Hosea warned *"you have eaten the fruit of deception"* (Hosea 10:13) because the people acted wickedly and depended on their own strength instead of the Lord.

Jesus said, *"Apart from me you can do nothing"* (John 15:5). It is deception to think that what we do just by human inspiration or insight counts in God's sight.

When we are self-dependent, we trust in our own "wisdom." This is also a form of self-deception.

Do not deceive yourselves. If any of you think you are wise by the standards of this age, you should become "fools" so that you may become wise. For the wisdom of the world is foolishness in God's sight.   (1 Corinthians 3:18–19)

All believers have to learn to view their circumstances as God sees them, and to see themselves through his perspective.

Believing only what we want to believe

When we choose to believe what is convenient or comfortable to us, we close our ears to what God is saying and our eyes to reality. Jeremiah gives us a good example. When Jerusalem was besieged by the Babylonians he warned:

This is what the LORD says: Do not deceive yourselves, thinking "The Babylonians will surely leave us." They will not!
(Jeremiah 37:9)

The people wanted to believe that they were safe, but they were not. When faced with difficulty or need, such as sickness, we want to believe the best outcome to the crisis. *Wanting to believe is not the same as faith.*

Faith responds to God's word, so those who walk by faith are not afraid to listen to him. They know he wants to bless and heal, but they are prepared to hear what he is speaking into the situation. Often there are things he wants to do before the supernatural answer to the prayer of faith.

Failing to listen to God or to obey

These are rebellious people, deceitful children, children unwilling to listen to the LORD's instruction.
(Isaiah 30:9)

Unwillingness to listen to what God is saying shows a desire to be deceived rather than to listen to and face the truth. This is especially the case for those who want an undemanding kind of Christianity.

There are some who listen to God, but refuse to do what he says. Disobedience is another form of self-deception.

> *Do not merely listen to the word, and so deceive yourselves. Do what it says.*
>
> (James 1:22)

Whatever God says has the full weight of his divine authority. *We insult him when we hear but do not obey.* This denies his Lordship over us. We hold our own views or desires as having greater weight than his!

Speaking negatively

James warned the believers:

> *Those who consider themselves religious and yet do not keep a tight rein on their tongues deceive themselves and their religion is worthless.*
>
> (James 1:26)

God is concerned more that we are right in our hearts with him and with others than that we perform religious duties. Negative words, gossip, slander, curses and doubting comments bring disrepute and damage the faith of other believers.

From the overflow of the heart the mouth speaks, Jesus taught (Matthew 12:34, Luke 6:45). Wrong words come from a wrong heart.

One way that we may speak negatively of others is to blame them for our own temptation and inclination to fall into sin.

Our sin is of our own making. A person only yields to temptation through his or her own evil desires. We conceive the sin in our mind; if we dwell upon it, we are likely to commit it. This is not God's good intention for us (see James 1:13–18).

It is deception to think that God has tempted us or wants us to be deceived in any way. He *supplies "every good and perfect gift"* (James 1:17).

Jesus prayed for Peter when Satan tried to sift him as wheat.

The Holy Spirit lives in us to enable us to resist temptation, and help us in our weakness. We must look to him for strength, and not try to put the responsibility on others.

Tolerating sin

This is common today and is even wrongly claimed by some to be a demonstration of love! We are called to love sinners by warning them of the danger they are in, not by accepting their sin.

> *Do you not know that the wicked will not inherit the kingdom of God? Do not be deceived: Neither the sexually immoral nor idolaters nor adulterers nor male prostitutes nor homosexual offenders nor thieves nor the greedy nor drunkards nor slanderers nor swindlers will inherit the kingdom of God.*
> (1 Corinthians 6:9–10)

Stating such truths openly is a quick way to become unpopular with the world and to invite opposition. Nevertheless, this is the truth, and believers have to stand up and be counted! We love the sinner, but not his sin. It is deception to claim that nothing can be done to change such people.

The gospel is the power of God for all those who believe, and is able to save them completely from homosexual compulsions, promiscuity or any other sin. Before the new birth, everybody is controlled by their sinful nature. The new birth gives believer a new nature and sets us free from the bondage of what we were previously.

Those who brush aside sin may also fall into the trap of believing everyone will go to heaven.

Scripture is clear about heaven:

> *Nothing impure will ever enter it, nor will anyone who does what is shameful or deceitful, but only those whose names are written in the Lamb's book of life.* (Revelation 21:27)

Only perfect people go to heaven! That is why we need a Savior, one who makes us worthy, acceptable, righteous and perfect in God's sight.

Believing false prophets

Jesus warned:

> *Watch out that no one deceives you.*   (Matthew 24:4)

False prophets claim to come or speak in the Lord's name, but speak things which oppose the truth. They make false predictions, which do not come to pass. We are to test everything and are to hold on to that which is good, not what comes from a false spirit.

Just because someone claims to speak in the Lord's name does not mean that he is doing so! False prophets are able to deceive because they can tell people things about themselves and predict the future. They counterfeit the genuine work of the Holy Spirit.

One of the most common forms of deception is for people to put their confidence in the messenger; if they do they will believe any message he brings whether it is true or false.

▶ *Because someone has said one thing that is accurate does not mean that you are to believe everything they say. Everything is to be tested.*

It is especially important to weigh someone's portrayal of Christ. Only the New Testament gives an accurate revelation of Jesus. We are not to listen to those who preach "another" Jesus, either by adding to the scriptural revelation concerning him or by detracting from it. Such preaching comes from "a different spirit," not the Holy Spirit.

Paul was concerned that:

Just as Eve was deceived by the serpent's cunning, your minds may somehow be led astray from your sincere and pure devotion to Christ.   (2 Corinthians 11:3)

An example of this is those who claim to be able to predict the second coming of Christ. Scripture is clear that God alone knows the timing of this event. Paul warns:

Don't let anyone deceive you in any way, for that day will not come until the rebellion occurs and the man of lawlessness is revealed, the man doomed to destruction.
(2 Thessalonians 2:3)

Jesus also warned that many would be deceived by those claiming to be the Christ. Many more have been deceived by those who endlessly speculate about the way to interpret the book of Revelation. They spend countless hours poring over time charts instead of getting on with the business of God's kingdom.

Anybody who predicts that he or she knows the exact timing of Jesus' return is obviously deceived. Only the Father knows that.

Being deceived by sin

Paul said, *"Sin, seizing the opportunity afforded by the commandment, deceived me"* (Romans 7:11). The law could tell him what to do, but not enable him to do it.

Now we have been set free from sin we are not to return to it. The writer to the Hebrews said:

But encourage one another daily as long as it is called Today, so that none of you may be hardened by sin's deceitfulness.
(Hebrews 3:13)

When you sin, your relationship with God is impaired, and so is your perception of the truth, for your sin is a denial of the truth.

Of course it is deception to believe that you can hide any sin from God. He knows your thoughts, your words before you speak them – and even how many hairs you have on your head! He knows everything about you. That is a threat if you are not walking in righteousness, but a joy if you are!

Those who are deceived tend to go on to deceive others. Paul warned:

> *Evildoers and impostors will go from bad to worse, deceiving and being deceived.*   (2 Timothy 3:13)

The way to avoid being deceived by such people is to *"continue in what you have learned and have become convinced of, because you know those from whom you learned it, and ... you have known the Holy Scriptures, which are able to make you wise for salvation through faith in Christ Jesus"* (2 Timothy 3:14–15).

Above all, unbelievers are deceived.

> *At one time we too were foolish, disobedient, deceived and enslaved by all kinds of passions and pleasures.*   (Titus 3:3)

We can rejoice in God's grace that has set us free from what we were. As we walk in the truth we will no longer live in deception. Pray for those who are blind to the truth and use the opportunities you are given to point them to Jesus.

Being deceived by wealth and the things of this world

In the parable of the sower, the seed of God's word fell among thorns. Jesus says that this represents:

> *"people who hear the word, but the worries of this life and the deceitfulness of wealth choke it, making it unfruitful."*
>   (Matthew 13:22)

Jesus does not condemn wealth itself, but warns against the way it can deceive people. Wealth can cause us to think we have no need for God, for we can buy everything we need. Nevertheless, material possessions will never satisfy our spiritual needs.

Wealthy believers find it more difficult to live trusting God, because they do not need to see him provide in the way that poorer Christians do. They may also be bound by their money and possessions, always concerned about looking after them.

The scriptures also warn us against trusting in worthless things.

Let them not deceive themselves by trusting what is worthless,
for they will get nothing in return. (Job 15:31)

The world puts its trust in riches and material possessions. Christians know their trust is in the Lord. He has given us the kingdom, which Jesus describes as the treasure hidden in a field, the pearl of great price. We should be prepared to sell all that we have to possess this kingdom.

If we seek first God's kingdom and righteousness in our lives, then he will take care of our every need (Matthew 6:33).

Do not be daunted by the number of different ways a believer can be deceived. If you walk in faith and obedience to God's word, you will escape every deception. The Holy Spirit of truth lives within you to guide you into all truth.

7

Speaking the truth

Because the deceiver is the father of lies, he will try to persuade you to contradict the truth about Jesus, about others and about yourself, by the things you say. This can be expressed in deliberate lies you tell or by a lack of knowledge or understanding of the truth. Either way, God is not glorified and you serve the enemy's purposes.

Lying is part of worldly living.

People all lie to their neighbors;
their flattering lips speak with deception. (Psalm 12:2)

Flattery has no place in the lives of Christians. We are to encourage each other with the truth, but not flatter with lies!

▶ **Christians are those who stand for the truth and are concerned always to speak the truth.**

A truthful witness does not deceive,
but a false witness pours out lies. (Proverbs 14:5)

Peter quoted Psalm 34:

Whoever among you would love life and see good days must keep your tongue from evil and your lips from deceitful speech.
(1 Peter 3:10)

Those who contend for the truth must expect opposition from those who are deceitful. David said:

> *People who are wicked and deceitful*
> *have opened their mouths against me;*
> *they have spoken against me with lying tongues.*
>
> (Psalm 109:2)

For this reason it is important not to be taken in by rumors about other believers. The devil has the habit of spreading false rumors, especially about those whom God uses in significant ways, in an attempt to undermine their witnesses. There are to be two or three witnesses before we listen. Remember, a witness is not someone who has heard the rumor, but who knows the facts!

> *Save me, O LORD, from lying lips*
> *and from deceitful tongues.*   (Psalm 120:2)

Christians should not do the devil's work for him. Yet often false rumors are spread by other believers. Be sure you are not one who does such things!

Even when you know a brother or sister has sinned, you are to seek to restore them, not to judge them. So pray for them, rather than criticizing or gossiping about them to others.

Jeremiah likens a deceitful tongue to a deadly arrow (Jeremiah 9:8). It is the enemy who fires these arrows at believers! God has armed us with the shield of faith with which we are able to quench all these fiery arrows. We must use it constantly and not allow ourselves to be adversely influenced by lies spoken about us, or wild accusations made against us.

The enemy uses these attacks to try to undermine our confidence, to put us on the defensive and to stir up resentful reactions. We shouldn't fall for any of these devices. We not only have the shield of faith, but also the sword of the Spirit, the word of God.

When falsely accused at his trial, Jesus said nothing. This is usually the best course, because God will always vindicate the truth.

There was a period in my own life when I knew many false things were being said about me in an attempt to influence others to turn against me. The Lord said to me at that disturbing time: "Colin, I know the truth, and you know the truth, and that is all that matters." I knew he would vindicate the truth, and that is precisely what happened.

At such times you can understand David's outburst:

> *Not a word from their mouth can be trusted;*
>   *their heart is filled with destruction.*
> *Their throat is an open grave;*
>   *with their tongue they speak deceit.*   (Psalm 5:9)

Yet David was able to take comfort in God's presence and power:

> *But let all who take refuge in you be glad;*
>   *let them ever sing for joy.*
> *Spread your protection over them,*
>   *that those who love your name may rejoice in you.*
>   (Psalm 5:11)

The truth is the answer to deception.

▶ **God does not condemn you for being deceived, but he does expect you to come back to the truth once you realize you have been deceived or have inadvertently deceived others.**

Ask the Lord to forgive you and make a fresh dedication of your life to him, to walk in the truth of his word.

Ensure that your conversation about yourself and others is true. Speak of yourself as the new creation in Christ Jesus that he has made you. You are not the person you were, but the new person you have become. The old is crucified with Christ and no longer lives. You live now by faith in Jesus who showed his love by giving himself for you.

You were taught, with regard to your former way of life, to put off your old self, which is being corrupted by its deceitful desires.

(Ephesians 4:22)

You do not put off the old self by endlessly looking at it, speaking about it, or trying to reform it! Because the old self was beyond such things, it was consigned to death with Jesus.

If you are a born-again believer, God's Spirit has come to live within your spirit. You have within you the spirit of love, of power, of a sound mind. You have the mind of Christ.

In your soul you have the natural mind, so you are still able to think your own thoughts and have your own ideas and opinions which can be totally opposed to God's word. It is in your natural mind that Satan seeks to deceive you as he did Eve, questioning what God says by his Spirit. You will be deceived if you fall into his trap by exalting your own thoughts above those of God himself, and exalting your own opinions above the revelation of truth given in the scriptures.

Christians who promote their own ideas will often claim to be led by the Holy Spirit. The only way to verify what they say is from the scriptures. The soul, even of Spirit-filled believers, can be influenced by deceiving spirits as well as by the Holy Spirit.

These deceiving spirits appeal to a person's pride. It has been the greatest sadness in my ministry to see certain leaders who had operated under genuine anointing and been greatly used by the Lord, suddenly change because they had come under the influence of deceiving spirits. Their previous humility suddenly disappeared and a pride arose in them which in time undermined their ministries.

Praise God that when people go wrong in such ways, he is eager to restore them, and it is a joy to see that work of restoration take place. However, the enemy knows that such periods of deception seriously damage a person's ministry.

Submit to the truth

Jesus at all times remained submissive to his Father. He made clear that he spoke no words of his own, only the words his Father gave him to speak. He did nothing on his own initiative, only what he saw his Father doing (John 5:19). He had not come to do his own will, but the will of the one who sent him.

▶ *Because Jesus remained perfectly submitted to the authority of his Father, he could not be deceived by the devil, but could exercise perfect authority over him.*

The same is true for every believer. If we keep ourselves submitted to God and his words of truth, we will not be deceived and will be able to speak and act with authority.

Jesus commended the centurion whose servant needed to be healed, because he understood authority. Jesus said that he had not seen such faith in all Israel – even among his own disciples (Luke 7:9)!

If you are prepared to submit yourself to God, you will submit yourself to his word, you will submit your thinking to his thinking, your ways to his ways. And this will keep you from being deceived.

So be careful about listening to prophetic words that appeal to your pride. That is not the way God works. He exalts the humble, but pulls down the proud.

The Spirit clearly says that in later times some will abandon the faith and follow deceiving spirits and things taught by demons.
(1 Timothy 4:1)

You do not want to be such a person!

Never fall into the trap of thinking that you could not be deceived. The enemy assigns deceiving spirits to attack every believer. All who are committed to pleasing the Lord are bound to be attacked in this way:

The seed on good soil stands for those with a noble and good heart, who hear the word, retain it, and by persevering produce a crop.   (Luke 8:15)

Walk in the truth

If you read the opening verses of the second and third letters of John, you will see a series of significant statements:

- He writes to those he loves *"in the truth."*

- He writes on behalf of *"all who know the truth."*

- He writes *"because of the truth."*

- This truth *"lives in us"* as believers.

- This truth *"will be with us for ever."*

- Grace, mercy and peace from the Father and Son *"will be with us in truth."*

- John rejoices in those who are *"walking in the truth."*

- His readers' souls are healthy because of their *"faithfulness to the truth."*

God calls each one of his children to such a walk of truth, even though others may misunderstand or deliberately oppose us. Jesus himself was accused of deceiving the people (John 7:12). However,

He committed no sin, and no deceit was found in his mouth.
                                        (1 Peter 2:22)

It is likely that people will accuse you falsely for your unwillingness to depart from the truth. Do not be disturbed by this.

Blessed are those
    whose sin the Lord does not count against them
    and in whose spirit is no deceit.   (Psalm 32:2)

The truth is never out of date. It is only the truth that can change human hearts, and change the standards of the society in which we live. There is no valid alternative to the gospel.

Our ability to communicate that gospel effectively to the world is dependent on our living out our message.

To walk in the truth is to walk in the light. Only light can destroy darkness. We want God's light to shine out of our lives that others may see we do the works of God. We want them to turn to him and give him glory.

8

Set free

By now it will be obvious to you that it is the truth that sets you free. As you live by the truth of God's word, you will be able to withstand the attempts of the enemy to deceive you.

However, it may be that as you have read this booklet, you have realized that in the past you have been deceived. You need to know the Lord's forgiveness and you need to stand against the devil's attacks, whether past or present.

There follows a simple form you can follow to help you to do this. Do not accuse yourself falsely. Act only on those things that are applicable to you personally. Do this prayerfully and sincerely from your heart, and then you will know that the Lord has forgiven you and you are separated completely from all former deception.

Where you have been wrong, admit this to the Lord; don't try to excuse yourself or blame others!

1. *Ask Jesus to forgive you for your ignorance of the words of scripture.* Agree to devote yourself to his words in future.

2. *Ask the Holy Spirit to show you areas of your thinking and believing where you have been deceived.* Remember that because of the nature of deception it is often difficult to see for yourself where you have been deceived.

3. *Confess these areas of deception and sin and ask the Lord for his forgiveness.* Remember, he does not condemn you, but wants you to know his grace and mercy.

4. *Check yourself against the list of ways Christians can be deceived,* as outlined in Chapter 6 of this booklet.

5. *Renounce all previous contact with occult activity,* if you have not already done so. You can simply say (preferably aloud): "In the name of Jesus Christ I renounce my involvement in ... I believe that I am set free by the blood of Jesus from every harmful effect these activities could have on my life."

6. *Destroy all charms, fetishes or insignia connected with the occult.* This will include any books on fortune-telling, palmistry, the use of tarot cards, etc.

7. *Renounce any involvement with spiritism or any other false religion or cult.* Ask the Lord to free your thinking from any false ideas of God that you have accumulated. Submit yourself to the truth of God's word so that your mind can be rescued.

8. *Renounce any involvement with Freemasonry* or any society that has involved you in praying to or making commitments to any other spiritual power other than Jesus Christ.

9. *Ask for the Lord's forgiveness if you constantly focus attention on yourself and your problems.* Face your responsibility for your sin and being the person you are, rather than blame others.

10. *Forgive any who have ever wronged you,* even those who have ministered to you in ways that have not directed you to the truth of your new life in Christ.

11. *Forgive any who have taught you incorrectly, preaching a Jesus less than the one of scripture.* Do not judge these false teachers: pray for them that they will come to a revelation of the truth.

12. *Renounce any involvement with meditation techniques that have their roots in eastern mysticism* (including yoga).

13. *Renounce any involvement with alternative medicines that have occult origins.* This will include acupuncture, healing through spiritualism, reflexology, etc.

14. *Consider if you have been caught up in unbalanced teaching that blames demons for everything that goes wrong in your life, or suggests that deliverance is the answer to every problem.* If this is so, receive the Lord's forgiveness and ask the Holy Spirit to bring you back to the right balance of scripture.

15. *Renounce any way in which you have allowed other people or activities to become more important to you than Jesus.* Ask the Lord to forgive you and bring your priorities into God's order.

16. *Ask yourself if there are any ways in which you want to be deceived because you do not want to face the demands of being a disciple of Jesus Christ.* If this is so, acknowledge it as a sin and ask for the Lord's forgiveness.

17. *Make a fresh surrender of your heart and life to Jesus.* Submit yourself afresh to live and walk in the truth.

18. *Praise Jesus for his love, grace and mercy. Thank him for the truth that sets you free.*

If you have enjoyed this book and would like to help us to send a copy of it and many other titles to needy pastors in the **Third World**, please write for further information or send your gift to:

Sovereign World Trust
PO Box 777, Tonbridge
Kent TN11 0ZS
United Kingdom

or to the **'Sovereign World'** distributor in your country.

Visit our website at **www.sovereign-world.org**
for a full range of Sovereign World books.